THE BIO-ILLOGICAL

Alan Bleakley

The Bio-illogical by Alan Bleakley
ISBN 978-1-7399003-3-5
copyright © 2023 Alan Bleakley

Acknowledgements

A Family Flagstone Rings with Our Steps, Nearly fish, first from birds, Nerines, Santra (Sweet-like, and Orange) and *The Soft-kissing of Adder and Dog* appeared in *The Manhattan Review* Vol 20 No 1 Fall/Winter 2021-22. The publisher wishes to thank the editor Philip Fried for his permission to reproduce these poems in this collection.

The cover artwork *Active Blood Platelets,* at the index *Signs of the Times* and at the endpaper *Untitled Metals,* are by Susan Bleakley www.susanbleakley.org.uk

Printed in the UK

Published by The Artel Press
www.theartelpress.co.uk

The Bio-illogical is dedicated to my life partner Sue and my loving family
— an endless source of inspiration

Alan Bleakley

INDEX

THE BIO-ILLOGICAL

FOR THAT WAY THEY STRENGTHEN THE BULB

"We should insist while there is still time" – Jack Gilbert

I searched for my father
through mental storm
over untold months
in a hunch that
he'd drowned in the fold
of the sheets and returned
to soil as a perishing corm.

At my back I heard
the unfolding ocean moving
ever closer to the shore
while ahead the darkening
horizon beckoned
at every stroke of the oar.

His death bowers my earthly
life and its bending talk:
"don't pick the flowers
never heedlessly tread on them,
leave them to die on the stalk"

THE BONES OF ANCIENT OTHERS
(THE ANATOMY LAB)

The bones of ancient others
As our root-beds.

There's sod for muscle and serpentine plant-
Root for tendon,

Flatiron stone for skull
And stope-shard for other bones.

Terra's chronic ptosis conceals
A cancelled culture: glyphs in quartz,

Racks of dead hunters,
Relics of bouled flint.

Now the moderns' flesh is stripped
Until the bones show,

The white dentistry grinning
Through it all.

Bodies as specimens
Ripped from the root-bed of their elders.

How will we save face
To re-tread their unpreserved steps?

A FAMILY FLAGSTONE RINGS WITH OUR STEPS
(AT THE DRAINING OF THE DAY)

I

The poet's thought-fox, a piss-line from pond
To coast, a stoat's huckstering and shallow
Gully, taut hare-string and adder's mark,
Turning sweetly as a well-oiled spit-roast.

Patterned by serial inflorescence
The route is clear, and I am at root.
I swank and billow; with strong back
I enter the earth, stitching as I burrow

My path sutured, the air resting on it
As hot as the bee's bite; I will wriggle
My way from here to there, if necessary
I will finger and furrow the coarse grass,

A bare-knuckle press raising light from ground
Spraying as I go, with cone focus,
Prow-muzzle steadied by weight of thought,
Instinct threaded by restraint, performed skin.

II

Half a mile from my house is a pond,
A mudsink, a fill of brindled water
Topped by toadspawn and purple pickerel.

If you walk in a straight line from the pond
To the west you'll pass my house and reach the coast,
Meeting fenced-off pasture, a grit-soused lane,

Nettlebeds underlaid with blue smalt,
Dandelion flowers hoarse from shouting, slanted
Roof slates (Davy's grey), granite and gorseflower

Hedge, lemon parsley beds, a bowing pine,
Stalls of brindled bushes, a hollybush
Tipped with minted growth; at cliff's edge, at day's end,

The horizon tightens on a shrinking
Green stopper that fails to plug the draining
Of the day, bleeding out into nightfall.

SANTRA (SWEET-LIKE, AND ORANGE)
AND THUNDER ON THE TUNDRA OF THE MIND

I derive from this ancient varnished
Knotted wrack a breathable salty air

I am gnawing at the roots of my desire
Like some saw-toothed wolverine

Solitarily loping the frozen subsoil
Of the mind - its acres, electric

With zoonotic illness, ready
To leap the gap of the species barrier.

...

A chip from a corner of frozen blanket
From which a chill gas visibly rises

In a brutally cold landscape entirely
Feigned, or the product of a circuit-breaker

Blue and smoking in shrill light, forcing
Me to breathe-in the ancient infection

That in imagination I call *Santra*,
Sweet orange, also a Roman cognomen,

A surname lit crimson, a pulp and rind
Fabricated from light dropping to sea

That can spark gas puffs from quiet tundra
And make them blaze with heavenly sounds.

I think this out loud and trek the landscape
As it crystallizes, can smell the underfoot
Crunch as it cloudforms and captures the light.

MAYDAY / MAY DAY!
THE BUTCHER STRIKES

I

Like a lover withdrawing anger
For the small mistakes in a green marriage

The holly tips soften from winter pricks -
They are as sea moss or cucumber flesh.

The woman's temper turns mint - she weeps,
Forgiving the poor aim of finger falls.

The man learns from the skin of the woman
Only to refuse the ghost of his birth caul,

The whispered code of the helmeted head:
"Clearing the wood tar to expose the bud."

II

Mother rabbits pull fur from their dewlaps
To line their nests crafted from nip and scratch.

And then, as sudden as temper, we are dead.
In my double-chinned grandfather's butcher's shop

Hanging rabbits drip from crosswise dewlap slits.
Cherry blood pits the newly raked sawdust floor.

Every evening at six we sweep away
The plain evidence of the butcher's strikes.

This smears all hope of resurrection:
Tomorrow brings an earthly shave at knifepoint.

THE HEART AS A BIRD ESCAPING A BURNING BUSH

Can you imagine a wagtail
With a tar-black heart
And a heavy head
Caught in a burning bush?

Of course not, although the knot
That is her heart
Must be heavy with grief
On every brief note of her song.

The human heart, a rib-caged oath,
Grows as a tangled bush of holly green,
Where a bursting fire can cinder
The holly head's rush of growth.

The heart can play away sometimes,
But will always come home to its bower,
A cradle for the crimson engine in the chest.
The locked box in which the heart rests

Is a holy chest fired dry and fired again,
A cindered mesh from which
The pied wagtail strides, guileless,
Its two-beat callow call now air made flesh.

OLD SKIN'S SHED

Whose hand had stripped clinkered blubber
From the hulls of beached vessels for decades,

Hoodwinking the old salts who judged his work
As worthless of recognition.

Would smell the lingering blubber staining
His fingers, as naked as duty of candour.

Strings old, stripped skin together as makeshift
Shed - for cover - for protection from insult,

The caul cast off in knowledge of hoodwink,
The hood cast off to parade the monk's tonsure,

The pate scrubbed clean for the pilot's kiss,
The pilot guiding the odd vessel into the safety

Of harbour - oh so slowly through a sea of sap,
A lapstrake boat glued to the standing weather.

An emergence from the caul as sticky as albumen,
Casts a glance towards shore taking in the tree-line.

In five extended points of exclamation
A stand of quaking aspen skinned,

These exclamations of nature whose silver skins
Wrap the slow ruminance of sap

Suck his doubting body from the clinkered vessel,
And re-lay his pressed skin sheet by sheet,

To re-build him from what is shed, as shed,
Or dry over-dwelling - his vessel drizzled around him.

QUESTIONS CONCERNING INDUSTRY STANDARDS

Brigid the wasp goddess, insistent
On making folksy inroads to my matter,

Dances at the spark-gap
Between her stinger

And my medial canthus
At the lip of the nasal bridge.

"I'm stung" -
Crisping an otherwise lax attention.

Did I offend you
Or were you simply careless in flight?

How to spetch the hurt? I stop dead
On the tarmac to rub the insulted palpebra.

The blame shifts.
Distracted by caterwauling,

Was it me who snatched the stab
Out of a day that otherwise fell as a gift

Like the softest of rain?

SUSSEX

The deities are sleeping in matter,
Their bedlinen chalk under which flumes race.

They are animals (of course) under whose skin
Pale wrappings of fat pulsate

In squat melancholic rhythms so that
The skin palpably ripples, so that

A gamy, plagued peace brews as if suddenly
These gods will grab us in nuchal gesture

To rub our faces in leather-scented oakmoss,
Then cap us with stony weights where we are,

Eye-to-eye with their toiling low-world
Lexicons, sensing a mishap – a red oil

Staining the stone, the celebratory thrum
Felt across the mass of its depression.

NATURE, READ

Red as the blush you throw as lure
Soft as the black bush after the flame
Red as the reel that follows the claw-cure

The dew-bird calling.

Echo – a single line:
Text me?

Crop until one word is left
Unread.

The cock crows
The chicken's craw swells
The eddy runs red & drains

The hen swelts, as hot
As the cock's passions

ZOOLOGY: DENATURED, NATURALLY CULTURAL

I

The most pressing of professions, I am
Keeper of my mother's breath (therein
            her face and instinct)
That fragrance held in her ashes with
The pelt smell of my Scottish father

The ashes long since scattered under rain
Stippling the tin-grey west Atlantic Sea
Its underbody in pseudocoma.

I would, counter-naturally, study
Animal cultures on the lumpy beds of granite-clotted
Cornish moors, earth stoppled by sacs of low
Cloud on leaden days threatening thunder.

I have no choice but to step out of this
World to join that of the animal
Familiars. It is a draw; no,
A compulsion – to be amongst them

Such as these leporids in a certain tense,
Pessimists held in the nervous present
Pinned by the presence of the buzzard's shadow.

II

My grandfather, a fat-pouched butcher
Double-chinned and cleft lipped, a flesh sculptor
Amorous as Jacob with his twelve sons,
His shop-ladder a stairway to hanging game,

The floor, royal yellow milled tree-flesh
Fresh from the sawmill, pitted by blood
Dripping from hanging meats; the familiar
Classless marriage of high meat and lowly

Sawdust blotter. A series of lintel hooks,
Rabbits and hares strung in clusters of ten.
Grandfather, I am in all tenses at once,
Nonverbal, naturally cultural,

Denatured and moth soft. The light
Of the occasion attracts me and
I rise, moth-boy, sawdust on my wings,
To flutter about the familiar hanging pelts
With their lingering meadowgrass odours.

It is like being in theatre.
I scatter more flaxen sawdust to blot the blood.

AGAINST THE GRASS
(MY FATHER IN MEDICAL CARE)

I put my ear to the grass:
how can the son blame the father?

When small he held my face to his face
and I could feel the burning
at his temples:
I worshipped there

And how things suddenly separate:
tenderize, fall apart, dissolve, burn off,
slip away, putrefy, and fall apart with a stink,
drift, split, unhinge, rip at the seams,
crumble, unhook, ripen and rot

Fathers running away to golden oils:
is that my father rinsing his wounds?

He is a fruit reborn in an abandoned orchard
his ashes made good
his voice flecked with gravel

I recognize the ruby overtones of his tartan dialect

THE SURGICAL LINE

the surgeons who repair through pain; sleight them
and they will crack one talus and dangle

you helpless in indignity; your best
protection is a sign of submission:

"I am unworthy of your resection"

THE SOFT-KISSING OF ADDER AND DOG

I

this one sunning on a rock slips away
at footfall; another that slid underfoot

rubs on pebbles rented by mint moss,
sloughs off parasites, sheds her scissored skin;

glistening undersnake emerges
brewing moderate poison; when her skin dries

her keeled scales in counter-looped coils hiss
one against another like water
            on a hot plate;

she seeks the pharmakon of common
nest and grave in sickly umber compost;

II

the deeper rot roots a surface hay scent,
a hanging steam from lemoning grass

is forked up, spawning fevered clouds from
my dipping prongs; deeper in the hot pile

the soundly coiled mother snake brooding
in the face of her brindled fate: to die

with a bellyfull of baby adders
sweating nascent poison as the mother peaks
            and dips;

III

whence a curious dog's damp nose quivers
at the compost cloudforms as the young snakes

burst out of the birth-skin deeper in the pile,
mother's split tongue lolling, a last taste of warm dung;

the dog's limbics follow the shapes of scents
her flaring nose strips pheromones from

compost clouds, she steps into a prepared
press of air, a parcel of brisket-breath,

sour hay smells smudged by the neolates'
extrusions, a tangle of ophidian

bane squirming in the mulch, all reflex,
with dog demanding inter-species alchemy,

she is transported by perfumes, stitched into
the alembic of her mind as the hooded

eyes of the adders, under that mulch,
inwardly wink in scaled recognition
of another.

THE REVERSE OF THE BUTTERFLY EFFECT:
AN ALCHEMICAL DIARY

"the body answering a pry with its own rejoinder" – William Carlos Williams

Prelude

The flapping of the moth's wings, the release
Of powders absorbing the blood trail
Of the lunar arc - signal changes
In the choices of movements of poisons.

First act: diagonal emissions

The flapping of a butterfly's wings
May cause a storm at sea, but the opposite
Is also true: I'll keep cropping from
The bee's text, until one word is left:
        Red

Second act: vertical drops

The belly of an incontinent sky
Hangs close to acres of zinc-skinned sea
Pressing it into pockets of resistance.
Irate local weather patterns spray out.

Third act: ground levellings

The weather-bubble an alembic
Of atmospherics; just metres-wide
This jacket of pressures, a whispering
Umwelt; under the weather-jar my mood
       tempers.

Fourth act: penetration

In turn, at the corner of my eye
Neeedlepoint, sting and running poison
Follow the bee's errancy, her flight thrown
By the elastic and weaving weather
        bubble.

The point of pain is like the sudden crack
Of a rimshot, the drummer's stick smarting
Against the metal of the snare drum;
Torment is registered in resonant

Movement across mitochondrial gel
As the muscular ventricles suddenly express
As the bee's stinger injects thunder
And lightning proteins - the skin around

My eye cockling from overprinted inks.

I'll keep cropping from
The bee's text, until one word is left:
        Read

THE MAN OF HARD CONSONANTS

with softer consequences
the branch sprang back to welt his
cheek, a corridored east wind
sniping at his fingers fumbling
with the willow scissors in
ulcerous rage; he curses, and
again, but the wide white
sky would not bleed while the willow
branch sprung back; his cheek split and
a bead of blood gathering
gravity tracing a plum red
trail on his willow white skin,
the blood bead flowers on his white shirt
wholly blessed, consonant and innocent

LET'S MAKE ROULADES OF OUR BOOKS AND EAT THEM WHOLE (ARTICULATIONS OF THE CHRONIC)

(for Shane Neilson)

I: rooting for returns

a specific articulation   of the chronic: hammer coming down
on nailhead over & over mingling metals in blistering devil-thwacks

the arm a blur, an exacting arc, lips elastic (screaming extremities)

backstage, a muscular storm is stewing   enters in costume,
unseen behind sheet-rain curtains

the strict separation of electrical charge (icy, crystallized positives drift
up, heavier negatives lump in the cloud-belly as hailstones)
under the tin-grey thunder-wrap
clap – one god's hand fist pumps another's – *clap, clap*

casts the world as shadow theatre, against which the hammer's
precisely
layered arc roots   driven into the same nail in the same spot

tic ... tic ...   a finger-blistering thump, runs in a rut,

a failed insertion of a central-line of slow-dripping regret, enveloped
by a rooted weather system.

In such illuminated theatre, all people appear as blood spots
In such illuminated theatre, everything that people do
                    can be read as blood sports

II: returning to roots

faced with the impenetrable (words & trees, where's the difference?)

confused by the overpowers of slow growth & phloemic girth
the loggers impulsively continue to swelt the eastern
hemlock growth with the fireslicing of saws & the hustle of chains,

the whole of New Brunswick pulped in an evening,
river systems choking with fibre, the land devolved
into its constituent parts, a deflowering

(the trees are our new-welted slaves, available for market)

& now within a root-marred space the man declares it
a clearing & sacred: here's redemption!
some kind of clearing of spotty debt alone with just a hammerswing
& its echoes

seeks to entwine habit & habitation, fashioning a particle factory
whose elemental prize is super-heavy oganesson;
disappears on production
in an instant (a fieldsong with call & no response)

(the chthonic gods we know have trouble hearing us,
their tympanic skins torn by the descent of thunder, digging in)

& so every slap of the hammer's face
is self-explanatory: the pinning of seemingly unpinnable weight,
& the making
of the medium of support, like whales in water.

the whales in the extra-tidal Bay of Fundy
transforming the man's insistent

shape-shifting thwacks into tonal iambics
(you can track the overtones in the currents, they run like threads
through the fabric of the woven water)

III: root extractions reveal the eternal return

the cure (old-time medicine) is the symptom itself, extracted,
not homeopathic but supra-pathic, treating difference with difference

the psychiatrist (frontstage, near to fainting
insistently rubbing at the sore)
says: you have a hammer with a claw

then why are you hammering in, rather than clawing out?
this is where the close fog rolls in as mystery roulades
the audience snoozes; the vaporous waste light pleads for transformation

(the copper kettle's dancing lid, kettle boiled dry, gas ring blazing,
kitchen abandoned)

the poet rids the stage of the conjurors
see – there is no nail there at all - you have
been hammering the hole where the nail

should be, or once was, but the hole
will never fill; it is permanently vacant
it is the hole-in-the-day through which Hermes Trickster slips, sly as fuck

IV: roots "on repeat"

meanwhile in New Brunswick the horses shit
while they're trotting & nobody gives a damn
while the tides of Fundy & the licking

St Lawrence spill onshore unsavoury gelatinous
matter tumbled in the lumina
of tiny waves; & the claw hammer
again lifts high above the spectred nail

365 IS MY NUMBER

(for Tolu Oloruntoba)

the white coat hanging in a twisted tree

and then the cotton unravelling and gushing
like a riverhead the pockets peeling
       let slip a tangled toolkit   each device
with its numinous wrapping unsnarling
and tipping into the gyre of the riven weave

the day's protective underskin of fat
       inscribed by habit wrapping the body-
without-organs is stripped out after
painful incisions to reach wringing hands

while out pops a sullen, underused liver
seeking redress and re-inscribing the colour
            of bruising

one apple fell from the tree   the apple's skin
was cracked and leathered and its dry core
had de-pipped to an empty broadcast...

it was you who loosened the white coat with your teeth:
sing 365 is my number... another year
in the name of Sanctious the Attritional

the waxy bedlinen stripped
the smell of piss and bleach
the hospital thrum
the glasswork everywhere smeared with spit, longing
and misery,   hope   too

here's medicine's butchered curriculum:

(the fat has melted and run off   it tangles in treetops
and screws with the information web of the medicine watchers)

Tips on how to hold a scalpel:
How: the scalpel tips
What: the tip of the scalpel
When: the scalpel at tipping point

scald the scalpel: shout it into submission
outflank it with poetry making the necessary
cuts through the skins of words

Where: the Pacific Northwest
(courtesy: Squamish, Musqueam and Tsleil-waututh placeholders,
re-distributors of wealth)

Transplant: 365 is my number   a new year...   a turn,
in the Constellation of the Ribcage
let the fat heart sing beneath the bone tent, I am tented with indigeneity

Upskilling: melt the scalpel blades and recast them
as pearl-coloured metal buttons:
one for your wife and one each for your children

see how the buttons shine after dusk
attracting the moths who mistake them for lost moons
(we are blessed by their collective understatement: the moths
have neither mouths nor fangs, nor claws... pincers or stingers)

box the tips of your anger and shake them out at the nightlights
they will mistake them for the knife-edge of afrobeat
neatly slicing the extended codas of Fela Kuti and King Sunny Adé
into single red notes   the single best treatment for scotopics
          transforming us into nightbirds or underearth wanderers

(the chthonic gods gave us the ring of truth but are hard of hearing
and so we must insistently shout)
but of course they are just pretending   deflecting

       while their emissaries sit at the chiasm right on the point
       of crossing of the optic nerves where sight refracts
(X marks the spot)

Let sight refract through the daily oils

Give us this day
       a day is enough to let the chorus ring
       one of 365
             "child how you grow!"

MY FATHER'S LIQUIDITY

Once I thought this a fat country,
Then my father's life was stiffed
By noisome disease we were not allowed to name.

What chance did he stand against kismet's stutter,
His tasselled limbs pre-figured
As hitch-knot to the blind ferryman's skiff?

He died under stale bedsheets
Apparently stripped of assets,
But when we pulled the sheets back

His capital body was floating in tow-coloured butter.

KEATS' LEXICON

Keats (alone and fevered)
his muscles growing hot
his gums bleeding

realises that poetry and medicine
share the same grain

with no wound to debride
Keats is soured in the broth of his own lungs

a once-springy moss spotted scarlet
each spot an exclamation

the terrain of pearled tissue
now a miracle farm of miniscule blood-oranges

THE ACCIDENTAL COMPANION

Distracted by a hum in the fold,
a car crashed, concertinaed,
and careened down a hillside
the driver recalling only the thrum
of the bee swarm - a hive in the head,
paradiddling on a snare drum

A deep-brain memory
of the entire human train
and its handiwork: thumping/
throwing / clubbing / making /
knapping / signing / keening

Once the hum subsided,
like a concertina with collapsed folds
the solid air was expelled
as coughed-up gravel,
the lungs rivelled

The bee swarm in the driver's head
dissipated, the promise of honey tomorrow
extirpated, the unexpected
rippling of the limbs accepted
in the softest of landings

Only then the drawing of the blind,
the uncanny absence of noise
a smell of cooking

not unlike an exclamation of dumplings
with silent fillings and rilled edges
basted by engine oil
as dark as blackbutt honey

THE FIRST STOMACH OF FOWLS

the farmyard soil
dressed with fowl dross

the sodality of the craw
scouring the cropless land

the wound skinned over
but still rankling at the core

HETEROPHYLLY

Midsummer's soft berets of holly tips
cap the hard heads where the thinking drips back
into the stems, and drains into soil, spent.

The soft holly hat, high, its lime rind
thinking ahead, urging chlorophyll
instants for its lower winter burst
of sharp tips; the waxing holly's mind

a connecting organ: air, sunlight,
dew, the earth-drawn juices, the green summer
berries loop into blush red punctuating

winter blizzards to drip into the eyes
of passersby as code for blood relations:

soft tops, thorn sharp under that; your mouth
will bleed out if you graze on raw gossip,
your body on which herbivores graze
uprooted from sharp habits of mind.

His head a gnarl, his mind a bloodied whorl
her sharp tips readily compressed in his flesh,

they compromise on the substance and weight
of mixed chlorophylls, red and green, orchards
of scholarship, fields of mutilation

mingle across seasons intimate
with the ingrowing drip of animal
continence, the fear of a dry stream bed
the under-cloud's silver raining on their crests.

The herbivores muster a collective noun,
a common strength as stomachs, in series.

NERINES

Sustaining summered minds
We are pollinators

Of the very idea
Of nerines - their sudden

Shout, the overcrowding,
The windwashed kissing heads:

Roseate, blush, coral,
Fuschia, salmon and rose;

Pickle- and parakeet-green
Compounds of stalks rooting

As sclerous clumps, ankle-
Knobbed garden flamingos

Heads pink as the day's end;
Alert, even wired,

On their raised beds - forests
Bursting from peanut-brown

Blisters fending off winter
As the year turns sallow.

PEARL

Where insult grits the oyster's flesh
A fresh pearl is burnished
By the very mesh it bruises,
And so a cult moon rises.

The bruised oyster's oils
Stain that anchored moon,
Once pristine in prismatic porcelain.

The whorled nacre not only affords
The pearl's iridescence, but also
Sprays music into the oyster's dome,
Filling the reverberatory furnace
With a measure of chordal moonlight.

A chemical called conchiolin
Is formed into a mooning bowed pochette
That sprays perfectly formed miniature chords
Against the ceiling of the mother shell
To bounce back as melody, tremolo and overtones,
The anchored moon seemingly jigging
In the great hall misted with music.

Love too is a mooning egg born of injury,
Sediment of compassion and compathy,
Wrapped in howls and pearling tears.

SKIFFLE

The day carved from corrugated tin
Noiseless as the leaden and ruminant air;

Sand, voicing the colour of a fruit-bowl'd,
Month-worn lemon against air as still

As the bedded adders coiled at back
In the beachgrass of the biddable dunes;

The draining rot of a near skeletal
Beached seal just shy of the high tide scud.

Is this the kingdom of the resplendent
Or the standard percussion of the washboard?

NEARLY FISH, FIRST FROM BIRD

I throw a net over whatever has been washed up
by an irritable sea
and pick over the spoils, hungry as a screech-gull;

the close stink of seal as it boisters
with the shorebreak
messaging something lyrical from its glistening skin

I swear it curled a lip before dipping down
to its salt orchard
its fish boroughs,

the sand, like dough
where the shorebreak laps;
the weather exhausts its changes

turns blank
for a precious moment the net releases
its fruits

I peck and pick at squam newly grown
I am nearly fish, first from bird

TAKING THE CURVES

The heart may be a glistening muscle
Blistered by pressures or a tired pump,

A fat-covered engine in the chest
Running down under a damp, bone grille;

But it is also a language, peppered
With stinking cusses and crosswise diction

As cursed as Job in its tireless strain
To make the next landing, or navigate

The next blind bend, a curve so perilous
That the heart itself races at its prospect.

DOES THIS MEAN LOVE HAS TOUCHED US?

Blood is sister to saltwater. The white shirt billowing
in the wind on the washing line has a red spot
where the heart would be.

Does this mean love has touched us?

A thunderstorm brews
the weather's dress folds tighten
at some distance a bellowing Titan rumbles.

Does this mean love has touched us?

She is in the habit of running her fingers
across my scalp. Perhaps feeling
for long departed hair in a task of exegesis

equivalent to a scriptural explanation.
Does this mean love has touched us,
as a kind of musicality on tap?

SOMETHING HOLY AND EXPANSIVE
(D.H. LAWRENCE AND FREIDA AT GWYNVER)

There is a long-stepped path hewn out of granite
Its bottom stone kisses the sand

It is limned with spoor - mostly dog and tangible
To dog - but also the scent trails of rabbit,
                    badger and occasional adder

The dunes carry the shame of impulsive affairs
Where dogs follow the scents of hurried sex

It is something holy and expansive

She felt the horn of the moon splinter

If he was the heft of the stone she was
Its physiology and unseen current

Quartz feldspar and mica sharing
The same slow pulse of expansion

The brindled dog's flaring nostrils rinsed with pleasure

AUGUST FESTIVAL

The tea-green holly's new bloom is headgrowth
of waxed paper; the cock crows from farmyard.

Nearby, the big-masked mummers walk out
Of bandaged sea, papersoft & salted white:

'The seaskin's split & pumping white blood
From its force & volume'; the lead mummer's

Legs straddling the holly bush: 'the sharps are
Overstated'; he's arcing at the bush's

Hardening headgrowth, these understated sharps
Already busy beading blood - his blood -

And that of his fellow mummers seeking
Women before the sharp winter crown

Spears all men and will surely bleed them
Like hanging white hares in the flooded

Salt-stained basement of the butcher's shop.
My Mummer-Grandpa's salted forehead in sharp contrast

To where all the red of the world has gathered
At hares' mouths in expressions of astonishment.

THE NOURISHMENT OF FRANK O'HARA'S LUNCH POEMS

The bourbon, sweating butterscotch,
lingers in the cobbled glass
this February Paris afternoon...

Solitude, rain, and Lutetian limestone roads
in the company of Frank O'Hara's *Lunch Poems*
("but I do not mean that tenderness
doesn't linger like a Paris afternoon").

The rain with no self-regard runs on and on,
stitching itself into the fabric of the quarried rock
("I don't know, I've stopped thinking, like a sled-dog"):

Wet cobbles
varnished by streetlight
"here I am on the sidewalk
under the moonlike lamplight".

O'Hara as heir to Vallejo
who says: "I will die in Paris, on a rainy day."
I am obsessed with the thought:
"how to cancel the calcium of stone",
the sediment that pools in my kidneys
as an interior cobbling.

The street cobbles kiss
under artificial light.

SPELLS

The curious boy in me
Stirs the wasp nest
Captures the stag beetle

And then is specimen
For the inquisitive gods

A pernicious lump pressed paper thin
By the weight of soil that comprises the sky
Is my burden

My head droops in shame
I carry this guilt of knowing something
Of which I cannot speak

'UNDER THE TIN-GREY THUNDER-WRAP'

The Artel Press
Liverpool